*Overcoming Rape, Sexual Abuse, and
Domestic Violence In Your Life*

Overcoming Rape, Sexual Abuse, and Domestic Violence In Your Life

—⁓—

Sharon Rose Walker

ISBN-13: 9780692649640
ISBN-10: 0692649646
Library of Congress Control Number: 2016903375
Sharon Rose Walker, Huntsville, AL

This book is dedicated to every man and woman who has endured sexual abuse or rape. The story I tell in these pages is based on my own experiences and shows how God brought me through these tragedies. Overcoming rape and sexual abuse is a choice you have to make. It doesn't just happen; at least, it didn't just happen to me. I pray as you read this book that the Holy Spirit rises up within you, and that you make the choice not to be a victim, but to be victorious—to overcome in the mighty name of Jesus.

And they overcame him by the blood of the Lamb and by the word of their testimony; and they did not love their lives so much as to shrink from death.
—Revelation 12:11, New International Version

Contents

Part One:

Overcoming Rape and Sexual Abuse

Introduction

If you've ever been a victim of rape, or attempted rape, you know that it is not simply a physical or sexual attack. You also know that it's not simply an act of violence. Rape is an act of violence that affects you emotionally, mentally, spiritually, physically, and sexually; it affects every fiber of your being. Rape lowers your level of trust, especially your level of trust in strangers and acquaintances. Rape also affects your self-esteem and self-confidence.

In my personal struggle to overcome the aftermath of rape, I was unable to find any help in the Christian community. Sexual abuse is a taboo subject among church folk. You go to church on Sunday mornings, people shake your hand and ask you how you are, and you put on a brave face. "I'm great!" you reply. Or you say, "I'm blessed! How are you?" And I love this one: "I'm too blessed to be stressed!" These are great responses—if only they were true.

Too many people who show a brave and happy face to the outside world are broken on the inside. Real life issues are usually not discussed in church. Rape is an important theme in the Bible, and its sitting on the pews, but no one wants to preach about it. No one wants to go to the altar to receive healing for rape; it's too embarrassing. We don't want our fellow Christians to know that we have been through something as devastating and personal as rape. So we go to church and go home as broken on the inside as before. We leave church without healing, deliverance, or peace, and we live with shame and emptiness.

I pray that you receive healing as you read this book. I pray that Jesus puts a holy boldness in you, moving you to speak out and help others who have been raped or suffered from an attack. No one in the Christian community should suffer alone as I did, wearing a mark of shame among people who seem to be perfect Christians.

We need to deal with these issues and receive the healing that Jesus has for us. It's not His will for you to live feeling hurt, scared, and all alone. It's time to stop feeling shame and taking the blame for what someone else did to you. What happened is NOT your fault. Jesus loves you, and Jesus wants you to be made whole. In John 5:6 NIV, Jesus asked the man who had been sick for thirty-eight years, "Do you want to get well?" The man gave Jesus an excuse; he said there was no one to help him into the pool. Today, you lose the excuse that there is no one to help you. Your answer is here. Through this book, God has enabled me to help you; and through this book, you WILL be healed in Jesus' name.

My Personal Experiences

When I look back over my childhood, I can't remember a time when I wasn't being sexually molested. I can't say for sure, but I believe it started when I was an infant. I remember one instance when I was in a car with my molester. I was about four years old at the time; we were living in Massachusetts. He asked me to come closer to him, and I slid over to the middle of the front seat. He slid his hand down the front of my shorts and into my panties, and started to feel me. I sat and stared at the car radio until it was over. At a very early age, I developed the ability to stare at something and focus on it so hard that nothing that was done or said to me could penetrate my mind. It's like my body was there, but I was far away. It was my way of withdrawing.

When I was about twelve years old, I got very sick. My mom took me to the pediatrician. Our regular doctor was out of town, so we used the pediatrician that our regular doctor's office recommended. During the exam, the doctor had me lie flat on the table. He stood near my pelvic area so he could block my mom's view. He slid his hand down my underwear and squeezed my privates. After we left the doctor's office with a diagnosis of pneumonia, I asked my mom why the doctor had felt my privates—I had pneumonia, not a vaginal infection. She said, "He's a doctor, and he can do that." It's sad to say, but sexual abuse was always a part of my life.

I never coped with it very well, but who would? I always had bad headaches and was constantly sick to my stomach. I was also a self-mutilator. Most people start self-mutilating in their early teens; I started in first grade. It wasn't something we talked about as a family, though my parents joked about it. I know now that they simply didn't realize that I was hurting emotionally. Neither did I. The physical pain of self-mutilation was much easier to deal with than the emotional pain of sexual abuse.

As a teenager, I dated very little. When I did date, I made sure it was with a guy who was "safe," someone I knew wouldn't "try" anything. My first boyfriend after college, Tom, was that sort of guy—we dated seriously for a year without having sex. After the relationship ended, he got an apartment. He wanted to have a party at his new place to celebrate, and he invited me to come. I didn't really want to go, because I didn't want him to think that we were going to get back together. But I decided to go for a little while to support him in his decision to get an apartment.

When I got to the party, everyone had already had a few, and they were feeling pretty happy. Tom took me around the apartment to see everything; he also took me into the bedroom. I was naive and assumed he wouldn't try anything. After all, we had never had sex when we were dating. He kept saying, "Sit down on the bed" (it was a water bed, and he wanted me to see what it was like). I kept saying that I didn't want to. I turned to leave the room, because he was getting very insistent about my sitting on the bed. We got into a shoving match, and he threw me on the bed, jumped on top of me, and tried to force me to have sex with him. I don't know how, but I was able to get out from underneath him and run out of the room and the apartment. That was the first time a man tried to rape me. I never saw this ex-boyfriend again.

When I turned twenty-five, I bought my first house. I had worked two jobs to put together the down payment. It was a small house on half an acre of land in the country. I was really excited and decided to have a housewarming party. My best friend at the time had a good-looking boyfriend who seemed to be a player. People came and went during the evening, but the boyfriend, John, stayed for the whole party. After everyone left, John was still there, waiting for his girlfriend to come (as it turned out, she'd had to work late and decided not to come to the party after all). John was on the sofa, and I was across the room, sitting on the floor. We were having a conversation, although I can't tell you what we were talking about. He stopped in midsentence and stepped over the coffee table with a strange look in his eyes and a scary expression on his face. I knew exactly what he was going to do. I started screaming "No!" In an instant, he was on top of me and was trying to get my jeans off. Thank God my jeans were too tight! As quickly as he started, he stopped. He got up, stepped back over the coffee table, sat down, and proceeded to finish the sentence that he had been in the middle of before the attack. Both of these attempted rapes happened before I knew Jesus as my Savior.

I have also endured an actual rape. One night, with my husband, our sexual intimacy turned into rape. What had started out as "normal" ended with him holding me down and me trying to fight him off. He was rough and aggressive. It was physically painful while it was happening and emotionally painful after it was over. It was nearly impossible for me to ever trust him again.

In 2003, God called me to start the Rose of Sharon Soup Kitchen and Thrift Store ministry. The early years were very hard, and the ministry and I struggled a lot financially. After I was evicted from several apartments, my mother invited me to move into her apartment with her. It was a blessing not to have to worry about paying rent.

My mother's neighbors were friendly and usually helped each other out. One of those neighbors was a man named Terry. He lived across the street from us for approximately two years, and he and I used to talk from time to time.

One night after riding my bike home from the soup kitchen (I didn't own a car), my mom informed me that my cat had been sick all day and had barely moved. I soon discovered that he had a high fever and needed to go to the pet ER in Huntsville. I couldn't carry a cat on my bike, so I asked Terry if he would drive us there. I told him I would give him gas money. He said, "Sure, jump on in the truck." I did, and he soon dropped the cat and me off at the pet ER. I offered him some cash, and he said, "No, don't worry about it. Call me when you're ready to go home, and I'll pick you up." I said, "It'll probably be a while. He's so sick they might keep him for the night. I can walk home." He said, "No, that's too dangerous. I'm going to be running some errands anyway, so just call me; it's no problem."

After my cat had seen the vet and been given antibiotics for his infection, I decided to call Terry. After all, I reasoned, he was out running errands anyway. He arrived within minutes of my call. He drove a four-door pickup truck. I put the cat carrier on the back seat and jumped into the front. But as soon as I sat down, I knew I had made a horrible mistake. He punched down on the gas and swerved this way and that as he drove; he had obviously been drinking, and he had gotten quite drunk. He was driving like a madman and pawing me at the same time. I kept shoving his hands away and telling him to keep them to himself. He kept telling me how I was going to "pay" for the ride. He drove down a dark alley. When the truck stopped, I jumped out and left the door open—I knew he would never chase me as long as the door was open on his precious truck. I opened the back door, grabbed the cat carrier, and started running. It was a miracle from God that he didn't catch up with me. I ran as fast as I could with the cat carrier toward one of the main roads in Huntsville.

This attack was more emotionally devastating to me than the others, because I was a Christian when it happened.

✍✍

You're Not the Only One

Rape has been happening since the beginning of time, always with the same devastating effects. The body heals quickly, but the emotional trauma lingers. Most people remain wounded for the rest of their lives if they don't make a concerted effort to be healed; that is a choice they make, whether they realize it or not.

Statistics from the National Sexual Violence Resource Center show that many people experience the devastating effects of rape and need to be healed:

1. Eight out of ten rapes are committed by someone the victim already knows.
2. One in ten women has been raped by their intimate partner.
3. One out of every five women has been raped.
4. One out of every seventy-one men has been raped.
5. Rape leads to depression, PTSD, alcohol and drug abuse, and even suicide.

The Bible also describes the devastating effects of rape. Genesis 19 tells the story of two angels who entered the city of Sodom to spend the night in the city square. Lot greeted them and invited them to spend the night at his house. We are told,

But before they retired for the night, all the men of Sodom, young and old, came from all over the city and surrounded the house. They shouted to Lot, "Where are the men who came to spend the night with you? Bring them out to us so we can have sex with them!"

So Lot stepped outside to talk to them, shutting the door behind him. "Please, my brothers," he begged, "don't do such a wicked thing. Look, I have two virgin daughters. Let me bring them out to you, and you can do with them as you wish. But please, leave these men alone, for they are my guests and are under my protection."

"Stand back!" they shouted. "This fellow came to town as an outsider, and now he's acting like our judge! We'll treat you far worse than those other men!" And they lunged toward Lot to break down the door.

But the two angels reached out, pulled Lot into the house, and bolted the door. Then they blinded all the men, young and old, who were at the door of the house, so they gave up trying to get inside.

Meanwhile, the angels questioned Lot. "Do you have any other relatives here in the city?" they asked. "Get them out of this place—your sons-in-law, sons, daughters, or anyone else. For we are about to destroy this city completely. The outcry against this place is so great it has reached the Lord, and He has sent us to destroy it." (Gen. 19:4–13) New Living Translation

This is the first instance of attempted homosexual rape in the Bible. I find it incredible that Lot would have preferred that the men of Sodom rape his own virgin daughters in place of the strangers. This shows the lack of value assigned to women at that time. But the angels got Lot and his virgin daughters to safety before God destroyed Sodom and Gomorrah. We are told,

Afterward Lot left Zoar because he was afraid of the people there, and he went to live in a cave in the mountains with his two daughters. One day the older daughter said to her sister, "There are no men left anywhere in this entire area, so we can't get married like everyone else. And our father will soon be too old to have children. Come, let's get him drunk with wine, and then we will have sex with him. That way we will preserve our family line through our father."

So that night they got him drunk with wine, and the older daughter went in and had intercourse with her father. He was unaware of her lying down or getting up again.

The next morning the older daughter said to her younger sister, "I had sex with our father last night. Let's get him drunk with wine again tonight, and you go in and have sex with him. That way we will preserve our family line through our father." So that night they got him drunk with wine again, and the younger daughter went in and had intercourse with him. As before, he was unaware of her lying down or getting up again.

As a result, both of Lot's daughters became pregnant by their own father. When the older daughter gave birth to a son, she named him Moab. He became the ancestor of the nation now known as Moabites. When the younger daughter gave birth to a son, she named him Ben-ammi. He became the ancestor of the nation now known as the Ammonites. (Gen. 19:30–38 NLT)

These two young women were the first female rapists in the Bible! They didn't understand that if they had prayed, God would have blessed them with husbands. Their lack of faith in God caused their two children to produce the Ammonite nation and the Moabite nation. Both of those nations tempted Israel to be unfaithful to God and His Word.

Judges 19 tells us about a woman who was gang-raped. The story begins with a concubine who got angry at her master and returned to her father's house. The man and his servant went after her and brought her back to his home. On the way back, they couldn't find a place to spend the night, so they decided to sleep in the town square. An old man from the town where they were staying was returning home from working in the fields, and he stopped and asked the men why they were staying in the town square. They said no one had taken them in for the night. The man told them to come home with him, and he would give them everything they needed. We are told,

While they were enjoying themselves, a crowd of troublemakers from the town surrounded the house. They began beating at the door and shouting to the old man, "Bring out the man who is staying with you so we can have sex with him."

The old man stepped outside to talk to them. "No, my brothers, don't do such an evil thing. For this man is a guest in my house, and such a thing would be shameful. Here, take my virgin daughter and this man's concubine. I will bring them out to you, and you can abuse them and do whatever you like. But don't do such a shameful thing to this man."

But they wouldn't listen to him. So the Levite took hold of his concubine and pushed her out the door. The men of the town abused her all night, taking turns raping her until morning. Finally, at dawn, they let her go. At daybreak, the woman returned to the house where her husband was staying. She collapsed at the door of the house and lay there until it was light.

When her husband opened the door to leave, there lay his concubine with her hands on the threshold. He said, "Get up! Let's go!" But there was no answer. So he put her body on his donkey and took her home.

When he got home, he took a knife and cut his concubine's body into twelve pieces. Then he sent one piece to each tribe throughout all the territory of Israel.

Everyone who saw it said, "Such a horrible crime has not been committed in all the time since Israel left Egypt. Think about it! What are we going to do? Who's going to speak up?" (Judg. 19:22–30 NLT)

This sad story of the gang-raped concubine shows the sick mentality of Israel at that time. People thought the rape of a man was a sin. But the host didn't think it was a sin for the concubine to be gang-raped through the night. Apparently, her husband—her supposed protector—agreed. I have to wonder if he got a good night's sleep that night.

What was wrong with that woman's husband? Why did he allow her to be gang-raped? When he opened the door in the morning and saw her lying there, he didn't say, "Are you OK?" No, he said, "Get up! Let's go!" What a callous and insensitive man!

Perhaps, on the way home, he reconsidered what had happened to his concubine. He apparently wanted all of Israel to know what had happened to her. He cut her body up into twelve pieces, and he sent the twelve pieces to the twelve tribes of Israel. How devastating to cut up her body. How horrible to box up the twelve pieces and ship them to twelve different tribes. How horrible that she died a tragic death and went without a proper burial and funeral!

Unfortunately, some men still consider women to be less human than themselves. Rapists definitely don't respect or value women. How can a man forcibly take sex from a woman and not care about the devastation to her body and mind? Ultimately, for the rapist, rape is an issue about control and power, and has nothing to do with sex. Thankfully, God does care about the victim. Thankfully, God considers women equal to men. As Galatians 3:28 NLT states: "There is no longer Jew or Gentile, slave or free, male and female. For you are all one in Christ Jesus."

Hurt

Men had hurt me sexually my entire life. Even before Terry had tried to rape me, I had trust issues caused by my sexual abuse as a child and the two previous attempted rapes. Would I ever be able to trust a man?

I've never liked to be hugged by anyone, male or female. Hugs have always seemed to be an opportunity to feel me up. Even in church, I have had men graze my breasts as they gave me a "brotherly" hug. I prefer a man to shake my hand and keep away from the rest of my body. I respect men who choose to keep their hands to themselves. In instances where a man just won't keep his hands off of me, I believe it is ok to establish boundaries, such as, "please don't touch me."

I've always known that men thought I was physically beautiful, especially when I was young. But I also always know that even if men wanted to be with me in bed, they didn't care about my thoughts or my feelings. To men, my intelligence and talents were unimportant. It seemed as though men could see my outside appearance but not the good qualities that God had put inside me.

To this day, I'm very cautious about getting into a car with a man. If it's not my husband, I prefer to have someone else riding in the car with us. Even if the man driving is a Christian, and even if I've known him for a while, I do NOT want to be alone in a car with him. Just getting into the backseat of a taxi with a male driver makes me uncomfortable. My thoughts immediately go to the what-ifs: What if the taxi driver doesn't take me to my destination? What if he decides to take a detour and rape me? This is when I simply have to trust the Lord to protect me.

Like most women who have been sexually abused, I went through a time when I slept with every man I dated. I would meet a man in a club and think he was Mr. Right, but I would discover in the morning that he was Mr. Wrong. Many women who have been sexually abused look for love in all the wrong places, as the song says. I was trying to use sex to find a husband—and that, as I discovered, is NOT how to find a caring, loving partner.

Although the Bible doesn't say so, I believe the Samaritan woman at the well was sexually abused both as a child and probably as an adult.

John 4:16–18 NLT tells this story:

"Go and get your husband," Jesus told her. "I don't have a husband," the woman replied. Jesus said, "You're right! You don't have a husband—for you have had five husbands, and you aren't even married to the man you're living with now. You certainly spoke the truth!"

In those days, it was scandalous for a woman to have been married that many times and to be living with a boyfriend. Such a situation could have come about only if she carried a lot of emotional baggage from bad experiences with men. The scars and wounds from sexual abuse or rape typically follow victims into every new relationship, even new acquaintanceships. Old wounds get reopened, or new wounds are formed, and the problems begin. What was once a minor anger problem becomes anger with rage and violence. Victims enter each new relationship with bigger wounds, and the emotional turmoil continues to grow and get worse. They become more and more crippled— broken emotionally, mentally, spiritually, and sexually—with each bad relationship, never finding the true love, compassion, and healing that they so desperately need.

IV

Disappointed in God and Myself

After the last attempted rape, I thought I would literally lose my mind. I blamed God, and I was very hurt and angry at Him. I felt like I was dying, emotionally and spiritually. I cried, and I cried out to God. Why had He allowed this to happen? Why? What was wrong with me? Was I even God's child? Did He even care?

I tried to pray, but I felt as if my prayers were hitting the ceiling and bouncing back at me. God was silent. Why wasn't He speaking? How had I failed Him? I was on the verge of turning my back on God. Going to the soup kitchen and to cook and serve meals to the homeless was a struggle. I felt I was near to having a mental breakdown. I knew I could not continue on this way—God had to help me.

The story of Tamar and her rape tells us about the devastation she felt:

Now David's son Absalom had a beautiful sister named Tamar. And Amnon, her half-bother, fell desperately in love with her. Amnon became so obsessed with Tamar that he became ill. She was a virgin, and Amnon thought he could never have her.

But Amnon had a very crafty friend—his cousin Jonadab. He was the son of David's brother Shimea. One day Jonadab said to Amnon, "What's the trouble? Why should the son of a king look so dejected morning after morning?"

So Amnon told him, "I am in love with Tamar, my brother Absalom's sister."

"Well," Jonadab said, "I'll tell you what to do. Go back to bed and pretend you are ill. When your father comes to see you, ask him to let Tamar come and prepare some food for you. Tell him you'll feel better if she prepares it as you watch and feeds you with her own hands."

So Amnon lay down and pretended to be sick. And when the king went to see him, Amnon asked him, "Please let my sister Tamar come and cook my favorite dish as I watch. Then I can eat it from her own hands." So David agreed and sent Tamar to Amnon's house to prepare some food for him.

When Tamar arrived at Amnon's house, she went to the place where he was lying down so he could watch her mix some dough. Then she baked his favorite dish for him. But when she set the serving tray before him, he refused to eat. "Everyone get out of here," Amnon told his servants. So they all left.

Then he said to Tamar, "Now bring the food into my bedroom and feed it to me here." So Tamar took his favorite dish to him. But as she was feeding him, he grabbed her and demanded, "Come to bed with me, my darling sister."

"No, my brother!" she cried. "Don't be foolish! Don't do this to me! Such wicked things aren't done in Israel. Where could I go in my shame? And you would be called one of the greatest fools in Israel. Please, just speak to the king about it, and he will let you marry me."

But Amnon wouldn't listen to her, and since he was stronger than she was, he raped her. Then suddenly Amnon's love turned to hate, and he hated her even more than he had loved her. "Get out of here!" he snarled at her.

"No, no!" Tamar cried, "Sending me away now is worse than what you've already done to me."

But Amnon wouldn't listen to her. He shouted for his servant and demanded, "Throw this woman out, and lock the door behind her!"

So the servant put her out and locked the door behind her. She was wearing a long, beautiful robe, as was the custom in those days for the king's virgin daughters. But now Tamar tore her robe and put ashes on her head. And then, with her face in her hands, she went away crying.

Her brother Absalom saw her and asked, "Is it true that Amnon has been with you? Well, my sister, keep quiet for now, since he's your brother. Don't you worry about it." So Tamar lived as a desolate woman in her brother Absalom's house. (2 Sam. 13:1–20, NLT)

The law at this time dictated a rapist should receive the death penalty. It is written in Deuteronomy 22:25–26 NIV, "But if the man meets the engaged woman out in the country, and he rapes her, then only the man must die. Do nothing to the young woman; she has committed no crime worthy of death. She is as innocent as a murder victim."

King David, who was Amnon's father, did not render this punishment. None of the men who violated me were ever judged in a courtroom or punished, either. But even if they had been, I don't believe anything would have changed for me. I believe that the hurt I felt and the animosity I bore men in general would have remained. It's possible that I might have felt some satisfaction in knowing that the offenders had had to pay for what they did to me; but I believe that the healing process would have been the same.

Approximately two years after Amnon raped Tamar, he was killed by Absalom's servants. We are told,

But Absalom kept on pressing the king until he finally agreed to let all his sons attend, including Amnon. So Absalom prepared a feast fit for a king. Absalom told his men, "Wait until Amnon gets drunk; then at my signal, kill him! Don't be afraid. I'm the one who has given the command. Take courage and do it!" So at Absalom's signal they murdered Amnon. Then the other sons of the king jumped on their mules and fled. (2 Sam. 13:27–29 NLT)

To fully understand the story, we need to understand the customs of that time. Tamar was a princess, the daughter of a king. A marriage would have been arranged for her when she was still a young child. As a royal princess and a virgin, she was closely watched. She would have lived in the women's quarters and would not have been allowed to go outside unless she was accompanied by other women and guards. Her situation would have been similar to that of the daughters of the president of the United States, who are always surrounded by secret service agents.

Although Amnon was in love with Tamar, she loved him only as a brother. Since she always had guards around her, it was next to impossible for Amnon to see her alone, never mind get her into his bedroom. But when Tamar's father sent her to Amnon's private quarters, she had no choice but to obey.

Tamar's struggling and pleading had no effect on her half-brother. She wasn't just fighting to keep from getting raped or to keep her virginity; she was fighting for her life. A woman of that time who wasn't a virgin was an unwanted woman. This rape ruined her chance at marriage and motherhood. Tamar went from being an adored princess to being an unwanted outcast, all because she was raped. And she bore that shame the rest of her life.

Although her brother Absalom was upset about the rape, he told her to "keep quiet for now, since he's your brother. Don't you worry about it" (2 Sam. 13:20 NLT). Really? Seriously? Why didn't he just tell her to take two aspirins and call him in the morning? Unfortunately, his response is typical. My own family acted as if my sexual abuse wasn't a big deal. They said, "You need to get over it," as if getting over it was easy. My own feelings were disregarded to protect the guilty. This is a sad and very common occurrence for survivors of sexual assault.

The attempted rapes in my life have made me feel disappointed in myself, and the shame I've felt was crippling at times. I've repeatedly replayed the situations in my mind. The would've, should've, and could've can be overwhelming.

I remember the first time I shared my testimony about the attempted rapes in a church setting. Someone asked me, "Why do you think so many men tried to rape you?" I wish I knew. Even Christians like to act as if the attacks were my fault. I don't have the answer, but, I do know that I am not responsible for anyone's behavior but my own.

I never heard a response from God. He never said, "You come across as a slut, Sharon!" I'm thankful for that, but I still ask the question. Maybe the answer is that someone who has been sexually abused as a child has an abused mentality, and she picks men who are similar to her abusers. Maybe I have developed friendships with men who share the same type of personality with those who have hurt me.

It's easy to sit around and wonder what you did wrong. But think about this: if you survived, you did all the right things. The worst thing a victim can do is to take the blame. Rapists are self-centered, egotistical maniacs who care only about their momentary satisfaction, which is the 'thrill' of power and control. They don't care about your physical or emotional pain. They care only about getting what they want. Refuse to accept blame for their behavior.

V

Anger

The anger and rage I've felt toward men has been over the top at times. Some days, I think to myself, "If one more man touches me, in any way, I am going to knock his teeth out!" Of course, this is NOT the godly way, but those are my thoughts; thankfully, they are not my actions. Again, with some people you have to establish boundary lines. "Thank you for not touching me" you tell someone who is violating your space.

I can't stand it if a man who doesn't know me touches my shoulder or puts his arm around me while talking to me. I always want to say, "Your mouth can operate without your hands on me!" Thankfully, the Holy Spirit doesn't allow me to say that. Instead, I try to back away, out of reach. Usually what he does then is move toward me in an attempt to keep on touching me. A lot of people feel that if they are touching you, they are making a connection with you—that you will be more likely to help them or understand their situation. It has the opposite effect on me. If a man touches my arm or shoulder, I become infuriated. There have been times when I have refused to help someone simply because he kept on touching me. God still has to help me daily.

Years ago, when my husband and I were involved in motorcycle ministry, a man came up to our group at an event and starting talking. He was an older gentleman and walked with a cane. He had a New England accent, which reminded me of my first abuser. The group slowly dispersed, and I was left talking with this older man. I decided to end the conversation quickly. I told him, "Nice talking to you, have a good day," and walked away. If Jesus wanted to save his soul, he would need to send someone else.

When I walked away, God spoke to me. He said, "You are prejudiced." I said, "No way, God. I'm white; that man was white, too. No prejudice there!" He said, "You are prejudiced." I said, "No, I'm not prejudiced!" God said, "You are prejudiced, Sharon." I said, "How? How am I prejudiced?" He said, "You think every man with a New England accent is like your abuser: an arrogant know-it-all—and a sex offender." He said, "Not everyone from New England is a child molester, and not everyone from New England is like your abuser!" Wow. What a wake-up call. Not only did I hate men. I hated ALL New Englanders because of ONE person! Because of one child molester, I hated everyone in six states!

It's amazing how God will reveal the deep hurts in your heart and the hatred and grudges that you unknowingly harbor inside! That day, God opened my eyes and delivered me from one part of the hatred I carried.

My anger toward others and toward life in general has been extreme. One day, when I was mad at my second husband, I went ballistic. I went into the kitchen and swept my arm across the countertop, knocking everything onto the floor. Then I walked over to the kitchen table and kicked one of the chairs down. As I was doing all this, I was screaming, yelling, and cussing. Neither of us was willing to clean up the mess, so it was four or five days before I went into the kitchen and picked everything up off the floor—including the chair.

Another sign of my out-of-control anger was my tendency to set fire to things. At one point in my life, I bought lighter fluid by the quart. I would keep four to six quarts of lighter fluid in my bedroom closet. If I tripped over the leg of a chair, I would drag the chair outside and set it on fire. One time, I could not get our new lawn mower started; I simply wasn't strong enough to pull the cord to turn the motor over. So I ran a rope from the starter cord on the mower to the bumper of my car. I jumped inside the car and kept popping the clutch, making the car lurch forward in an attempt to start the motor. I know—it was crazy. Anyway, I couldn't get the mower to start, so it ended up in the burn pit. My husband rescued the mower from the fire.

Another time, our used Honda Accord was my target. The car ran fine for my husband, but not for me. Every time I drove it, the motor would turn off two or three miles from our house, and I was never able to get it started again. But when help arrived, the car would always—and I mean ALWAYS—start for whoever had come to my rescue. The last time I drove the car, I told my husband, "If that car turns itself off on me again, I'm going to set it on fire on the side of the road!" He knew I would do it, so he never let me have the car keys again.

My healing from men in general has been a long and slow process. Overall, I'm much better than I used to be, but I'm not where God wants me to be. Most days, I'm fine with men. But it only takes one man trying to touch me when he shouldn't to make me mad. Sometimes, I wish I were wearing a T-shirt that says, "Unless you want to get clobbered, do not touch me!"

Yes, I continually remind myself of the fruits of the Holy Spirit. As Galatians 5:22–23 NLT says, "But the Holy Spirit produces this kind of fruit in our lives: love, joy, peace, patience, kindness, goodness, faithfulness, gentleness, and self-control. There is no law against these things."

There are instances, especially with previous abusers, when the only fruits of the Holy Spirit you can show them are peace, patience, and self-control. You can show other gifts of the Holy Spirit to a previous abuser, but you have to be cautious when you do. You don't want the abuser to think, "Hey, she liked it!"

I can remember my rapist neighbor calling out to me after the attempted rape, "Hey, you want some of this?" He continued to live across the street from me for about six months after the assault, and whenever he saw me, he always had a sexual comment. I would walk in the other direction, thanking God for His protection over me and praying that He would save, heal, and deliver my neighbor from sexual perversion in the mighty name of Jesus.

❧

Depression

I have struggled with depression my entire life. Growing up, I was either angry, self-mutilating, depressed—or all of the above. At times, I felt like a walking time bomb. When God saved my soul, I was one of the most messed-up people on earth. I was on my second marriage, and I grew and smoked marijuana several times a day. I drank and cussed worse than any sailor ever considered doing. I had panic attacks. My husband and I had a very volatile relationship, and the marriage didn't last.

Because of depression and panic attacks, I was on Prozac. I remember trying to drive home from work one day and feeling as if every car that passed me was trying to run me off the road. It was a bizarre experience. I had to pull over to the side of the road to calm down and convince myself that nobody was after me. It was a sign of my poor mental state.

Even after I became a Christian, I was on medication for years. I didn't get wounded overnight, and God didn't heal me overnight, either. Many times, I went to the altar for prayer and left feeling healed and whole. Then, sometime later, God would show me that I had another issue in my heart to deal with.

Once, my pastor and some of the other church members were going to a revival service a few hours away. Everyone kept inviting me to go, but I didn't feel like going. The day of the revival, my husband and I were fighting, and I knew if I stayed home that night, I would be miserable. So I decided to go the service. I'm glad I did, because that revival changed me forever. The preacher was amazing and very anointed. He preached on sexual abuse. He told a story about his wife and her sexual abuse. He told stories that were very similar to my own experiences, and I cried through most of the message. At altar call, he said, "If you were sexually abused as a child, come up. I want to pray for you." I was one of the first people at the altar.

Tears were streaming down my face. I was crying so hard that I couldn't speak. The preacher grabbed me by my head and said, "Can you see him?" I shook my head yes. He said, "Can you see his face?" I cried out, "Yeessss!" He said, "FORGIVE HIM!" He let my head go and went to the next person. That was all it took. Forgiving my abusers had been a huge obstacle for me. But that night God healed my heart in a huge way. I finally felt free.

When I woke up the next morning, I felt different. I felt good but strange. It was a feeling I had never felt before. I couldn't figure it out, how I felt so different and so good at the same time. Finally, I realized that my heart didn't hurt. My heart DIDN'T HURT! I had never experienced that before. I was thirty-five years old, and finally my heart didn't hurt! Thank you, Jesus!

I am convinced that receiving healing from the Lord is an absolute must. At the same time, our attitude is a huge part of our healing.

The words of these psalms are inspirational:

Why am I discouraged? Why is my heart so sad? I will put my hope in God! I will praise Him again—my Savior and my God! Now I am deeply discouraged, but I will remember You—even from distant Mount Hermon, the source of Jordan, from the land of Mount Mizar. I hear the tumult of the raging seas as Your waves and surging tides sweep over me. But each day the Lord pours His unfailing love upon me, and through each night I sing His songs, praying to God who gives life. (Ps. 42:5–8 NLT)

"O God, my rock," I cry, "Why must I wander around in grief, oppressed by my enemies?" Their taunts break my bones. They scoff, "Where is this God of yours?" Why am I discouraged? Why is my heart so sad? I will put my hope in God! I will praise Him again—my Savior and my God! (Ps. 42:9–11 NLT)

We are told in Romans 12:2 NLT "Don't copy the behavior and customs of this world, but let God transform you into a new person by changing the way you think. Then you will learn to know God's will for you, which is good and pleasing and perfect."

A big part of my healing came from choosing to change the way I think. I had to CHOOSE to stop reliving the past in my mind on a continual basis. The only thing that continually reliving the past does is bring you down; it causes you to relive DAILY the pain you endured. It's very difficult to be healed when you continue living in the past. One time I heard a preacher say, "Why is the windshield in your car so big, and the rearview mirror so small? Because where you are going is much more important than where you have been!" That is a very profound statement.

Consider Paul's crucial words:

No, dear brothers and sisters, I have not achieved it, but I focus on this one thing: Forgetting the past and looking forward to what lies ahead. I press on to reach the end of the race and receive the heavenly prize for which God, through Christ Jesus, is calling us. (Philippians. 3:13–14 NLT)

Forgetting the past and looking forward to what lies ahead is not easy to do. It will take time and practice. When you realize you're reliving an abuse in your mind, rebuke it in the name of Jesus, and start thinking about what you want in the future. It took me a long time to be able to do this. Being negative, withholding forgiveness, and living in the past were ingrained in me. That's how I grew up. My family was always negative; if people did something to offend you—well, you always hated them and never forgave them. We talked constantly about the past and rarely about the future. I realize now what a sad life we lived.

Up until the day she died, my mom had a long list of friends and family members she hated and wasn't speaking to. Many times, my mom wasn't speaking to me. If I didn't do what she wanted me to do, I wasn't worth speaking to. When I was a child, she gave me the silent treatment for days at a time.

When I got older, she could go weeks without speaking to me. Once I became an adult, she sometimes went months without speaking a kind word to me. If I called her on the phone when she was angry with me, I had to do most of the talking, and I would get only short yes and no answers back. If I could ask her one question now, it would be "Was it worth it? Was it worth all the hatred?" She died a sad, angry, bitter, and very lonely person. That's not how I choose to live and die. Thankfully, Jesus has delivered me of these things.

I've often wondered why I suffered from sexual abuse at the hands of men—why God didn't prevent it from happening. Maybe if these things had not happened, I would never have been saved. I might never have experienced the love of Christ or healing from heaven above. If these things had never happened to me, I wouldn't understand people who have been sexually abused.

The Bible speaks to this possibility:

Jesus answered them, "Healthy people don't need a doctor—sick people do. I have come to call not those who think they are righteous, but those who know they are sinners and need to repent." (Luke 5:31–32 NLT)

I believe that first part of Jesus's reply is my answer. If I hadn't been abused, if I hadn't been emotionally sick, I never would have needed Jesus. But because of the trauma in my life, I needed a Savior; I needed healing; I needed deliverance.

Once I really started seeking God for healing, He healed me in stages. I started asking the Lord to let me know when it was OK for me to get off Prozac—I didn't want to be on it my entire life. When the Lord let me know it was time to stop, I went to the doctor to ask him how to wean myself off Prozac. He laughed at me and said, "You don't need less Prozac, you need MORE Prozac!" He then increased the dosage. I thought, "Well, maybe I didn't hear from the Lord!" That's what the devil does; he convinces you that you never heard from God. Anyway, for the next month, I took the higher dosage of Prozac, but I realized that I didn't feel any better! So I told the Lord, "OK, God. I listened to the doctor and took more medicine, but it didn't help me feel better. The doctor also told me I would always be on medication—that I could never be without it. Please, Jesus, tell me how to safely get off of this medication." God is amazing. He answered my prayer. When it was time to back away from the medicine, the Holy Spirit stopped me from taking a pill. First, He stopped the nighttime dosage; then, I was only taking it in the mornings. Eventually, I was taking Prozac every third morning. Then, one day, the Holy Spirit said, "Stop" when I went to take a pill. I have been off Prozac since 2001, praise God. I am very thankful for God's healing power!

VII

How I Overcame

After Terry tried to rape me, I nearly lost my mind—and my salvation. One day, I realized the best thing I could do would be to write a letter to every man who had ever abused me. I needed to put what each man had done into words and to counteract his behavior with the Word of God. This letter was written shortly after the last attack, and unfortunately, I still had a victim mentality. I want you to see the letter how it was originally written, although, if I wrote it now, it would sound victorious. God used this letter to bring healing into my life. Here is my letter.

September 23, 2005
To: Every man who has ever violated me
From: The woman you tried to destroy

You have used me and abused me sexually. Three of you attempted to rape me. Two of those times were before I was saved, and I can look back now and say that maybe I was dressed inappropriately, or that I led you on, or that I was somewhere I should not have been. I have always put the blame on myself for your stupid behavior. But on September 21, 2005, I was saved, I am a woman of God. I do not allow myself to be alone with men or get myself into questionable or potentially immoral situations. I live according to the Word of God, both in public and in private. I will NOT accept the blame for your behavior.

Job 27:3–6 says, "As long as I have life within me, the breath of God in my nostrils, my lips will not speak wickedness, and my tongue will utter no deceit. I will never admit you are in the right. As long as I live, I will not deny my integrity. I will maintain my righteousness and never let go of it; my conscience will not reproach me as long as I live."

You have repeatedly tried to make me the victim. But now I say with 1 Corinthians 15:57 NIV, "Thanks be to God! He gives us the victory through our Lord Jesus Christ." Sometimes it seems I have overcome my feelings of anger and resentment toward you, and then you do something else to cause me to fall. But now I say with Micah 7:8 NIV, "Do not gloat over me, my enemy! Though I have fallen, I will rise. Though I sit in darkness, the Lord will be my light."

Why would you want to take something that is not for you to have? Why would you want sex when the other person doesn't want it? I don't want you; I never did. You don't have the capability to be a lover to me, so you could never be a husband. Isaiah 54:5 NIV says, "For your Maker is your husband—the Lord Almighty is his name—the Holy One of Israel is your Redeemer; he is called the God of all the earth."

John 10:10 NIV says, "The thief comes only to steal and kill and destroy; I have come that they may have life, and have it to the full."

You have tried to steal the calling that God has on my life. Romans 11:29 NIV says, "For God's gifts and his call are irrevocable." Devil, you have wasted your time.

You have tried to kill who I am. Jeremiah 1:4–5 NIV says, "The Word of the Lord came to me saying, 'Before I formed you in the womb I knew you, before you were born I set you apart; I appointed you as a prophet to the nations.' Devil, you can't kill who God said I am before I was even in the womb!"

You have tried to destroy me by labeling me a victim. Romans 12:21NIV says, "Do not be overcome by evil, but overcome evil with good." 1 John 5:4 NIV says, "For everyone born of God overcomes the world." John 16:33 NIV says, "I have told you these things, so that in me you may have peace. In the world you will have trouble. But take heart! I have overcome the world." No matter what harm you try to bring my way, devil, I will NOT be the victim, I AM THE VICTOR!

You have tried repeatedly to destroy me. Your last attempt was rape—and it failed. Isaiah 54:17 NIV says, "No weapon forged against you will prevail, and you will refute every tongue that accuses you. This is the heritage of the servants of the Lord, and this is their vindication from me, declares the Lord. No weapon formed against you shall prosper." That is why the Lord made a way for me to escape! YOU CAN'T WIN! 2 Timothy 4:17–18 NIV says, "But the Lord stood at my side and gave me strength, so that through me the message might be fully proclaimed and all the Gentiles might hear it. And I was delivered from the lion's mouth. The Lord will rescue me from every evil attack and bring me safely to His heavenly kingdom. To Him be glory forever and ever. Amen."

Now, I MUST forgive you. I have to let this hurt go. But I will not forget you or what you tried to do to me. This is my testimony. God brought me through. I can hear Jesus say, "Let's go to the other side" Luke 8:22–25 NIV. Jesus is telling me, "Let's go to the other side of life. Let's leave these troubles here and go to the side where the blessings of God are." I also think of Psalm 40:2 NIV: "He lifted me out of the slimy pit, out of the mud and mire; he set my feet on a rock and gave me a firm place to stand." Psalm 113:7 NIV says, "He raises the poor from the dust and lifts the needy from the ash heap; he seats them with princess, with the princes of their people."

You cannot have me, devil! I will NEVER give in to you. Here are twenty-two reasons why:

1. I am an overcomer by the blood of the Lamb and the word of my testimony. (Rev. 12:11 NIV)
2. I am more than a conqueror through Him who loves me. (Rom. 8:37 NIV)
3. Greater is He that is in me than he that is in the world. (1 John 4:4 NIV)

4. God has delivered me from the evil one. (Matt. 6:13 NIV)
5. I have power and authority to overcome the enemy. (Luke 10:19 NIV)
6. Nothing can separate me from the love of God. (Rom. 8:38 NIV)
7. I cannot be snatched out of His hand. (John 10:28 NIV)
8. I have faith that moves mountains. (1 Cor. 13:2 NIV)
9. I am complete and lack nothing. (James 1:4 NIV)
10. I am blessed in the city and blessed in the country. (Deut. 28:3 NIV)
11. I am blessed when I come in and blessed when I go out. (Deut. 28:6 NIV)
12. I am the head and not the tail. (Deut. 28:13 NIV)
13. I am the lender and not the borrower. (Deut. 28:12 NIV)
14. Everything I put my hand to prospers. (Deut. 28:12 NIV)
15. God has set me above my companions. (Ps. 45:7 NIV)
16. I am a good soldier, standing firm on the solid Rock. (Eph. 6:11–18 NIV)
17. I am called, chosen, and faithful. (Rev. 17:14 NIV)
18. I will speak of God's statutes before kings. (Ps. 119:46 NIV)
19. I am anointed with the oil of joy. (Ps. 45:7 NIV)
20. I am anointed to comfort, proclaim freedom, heal, and preach. (Isa. 61:1–2 NIV)
21. I am a prophet to the nations. (Jer. 1:5 NIV)
22. I am a fortified city, an iron pillar, and a bronze wall. (Jer. 1:18 NIV)

The Bible says, "Touch not my anointed and do my prophets no harm" (Ps. 105:15 NIV). In the words of Jesus, my prayer is this: Forgive them, Father, for they know not what they do" (Luke 23:34 NIV). I can hear God say, "I am bringing my righteousness near, it is not far away; and my salvation will not be delayed. I will grant salvation to Zion, my splendor to Israel. Amen" (Isa. 46:13 NIV).

Signed,
A Woman of God with the Victory,
Sharon Rose Walker

VIII

How to Overcome

As I have previously stated, overcoming rape and sexual abuse is a choice. For over thirty years, I lived as a victim. A male friend told me one day, "Sharon, you have battered woman syndrome." It was true, but I didn't have to wallow in it. God wants us to turn away from being victims and realize that we can be victorious.

After the last attempted rape, I needed some real help. Unfortunately, it's hard to find anyone who will discuss rape in the Christian community. One pastor told me that I needed to forgive my abusers, but he didn't offer to pray with me or counsel me. He didn't even suggest where I might get some real help. The Christian community needs to stop sticking their heads in the sand. People need help; they need prayer; they need healing and deliverance. Sexual assault and rape are issues we need to deal with; we have to stop acting as if we are so holy and so perfect that nothing bad has ever happened to us.

When people tell me about rape, sexual abuse, or attempted rape in their lives, I always share with them the letter I wrote to my abusers. After I wrote the letter, I read it aloud four or five times a day for weeks. I needed to get it into my spirit. I needed to reprogram my mind, my self-esteem, my self-confidence, and my self-worth. I needed to undo the brainwashing. You probably do, too. As the weeks went by, I could feel myself getting stronger; I was getting better each time I read the letter aloud. As time went by and I continued to feel better, I read the letter less often.

Write your own letter to your abusers. Let your abusers know what they tried to do to you, and rebuke it using the Word of God. By searching out scripture, you will learn a lot about God and His Word. You will also have to deal with your own feelings. This is the best way I know to overcome rape and sexual abuse.

It will take time for you to feel whole. Be encouraged. God has healing for you. Seek Him daily in prayer and in reading His word. 1 Peter 2:24 says, "He personally carried our sins in His body on the cross so that we can be dead to sin and live for what is right. By His wounds you are healed." Did you catch that? YOU ARE HEALED by His wounds! I am praying for you, in the mighty name of Jesus!

Part Two:

Overcoming Domestic Violence

My Personal Experience

In 1993, I met a man I thought was the man of my dreams. He was good looking, had a sense of humor, and was a few years younger than I was. We seemed to hit it off right from the beginning. I was thirty-one and still into the rock-and-roll look, which he definitely had. We would talk for hours on the phone.

I was going through a divorce from my first husband, who was going to be taking our car with him when he moved out. I lived thirty minutes away from work and was very concerned about getting a vehicle. Right before my husband moved out, this good-looking dream man asked me out on a date. I will never forget his telling me, "Sharon, I'll buy you a car." I said, "You don't even know me! What if it doesn't work out between us?" He said the sweetest thing a man has ever said to me. "To go out with you, even for one night, is worth the cost of a car. You can keep it." That was all it took. I was hooked.

Neither one of us was saved or cared anything about knowing the Lord. My first husband moved out on a Sunday, and my new man came for dinner on Monday and never went back home.

We lived together for almost a year before we got married. We drank, smoked pot, and grew our own dope. For our wedding, we went to the courthouse. After we said our vows, we went to the car, rolled up a joint, and smoked pot all the way to Chattanooga, Tennessee. We rented a motel with a hot tub, and we drank and smoked pot all weekend.

During our first year of marriage, we both got saved. We were really on fire for the Lord. We went to a church near our house and started serving there. I played guitar as a member of the Praise and Worship Team, and my husband and I taught a Sunday school class for teens. Although no one knew it, we were still pot smokers at the time. Our deliverance came later.

At this point in our marriage, I can say that he was a good man and a good husband. We both worked full time and lived paycheck to paycheck, but we were happy. The abuse didn't start until years later.

In 1997, we decided to sell the house I owned, buy a piece of land, and put a trailer on it. The house we were living in was 500 square feet, and the trailer was 1,280. His daughter was living with us part time, and we needed extra space and an extra bathroom. Since our new home was forty minutes away from our old church, we decided to find a new one.

We quickly found a church we liked, and I soon began playing guitar as a member of the Praise and Worship Team. But after about six months, he started missing services. "I'm not going," he began to tell me on Sunday mornings. "I don't owe those people anything." I would try to convince him to go, but more and more often, he decided to stay home.

During this time, something changed in him. All I can tell you is that the Bible says that when you cast a demon out of someone, that person needs to receive the Holy Spirit. Otherwise, the devil will come back—and when it does, the person will behave seven times worse than before. Matthew 12:45 says, "Then the spirit finds seven other spirits more evil than itself, and they all enter the person and live there. And so that person is worse off than before. That will be the experience of this evil generation."

My second husband and I had been living in the trailer for about a year when his grandmother died, and he decided he wanted to sell it and buy her house. Any time you decide to buy a house, you take on more stress—the process of getting a mortgage is intense. Between leaving the church and going through the house-buying process, my husband was becoming a very nasty person to live with. I kept hoping that once we bought the house and moved in, he would return to being the nice man I married.

After we moved into the house, things escalated to the point of no return. My husband became violent and very unpredictable, and my life became a living hell. I was verbally and physically abused—I felt as if were constantly walking on eggshells. Being alone, I began to realize, is better than being with the wrong person.

Physical Abuse

Physical abuse can include beating, biting, choking, grabbing, hitting, kicking, pinching, pulling hair, smothering, spanking, twisting arms, slapping, shoving, shaking, scratching, restraining, punching, and more. My husband grabbed, hit, slapped, and shoved me during the remaining four years of our marriage—and whatever he did to me, I did right back. I refused to accept his abuse without a fight. One day, he said to me, "I don't know why you're so mad at me; I didn't hit you very hard." I said, "Well, when I run over you with my car, I won't run over you very hard!"

One day when we were arguing, he came up to me, grabbed the collar of my shirt, and started jerking it up and down hard and fast. So I grabbed his shirt and started doing the same. Unfortunately, all this did was add fuel to the fire.

One thing I have learned about violent men is that they are irrational. When I reciprocated his abuse, it made him madder than ever. Not once did he apply reason to the situation. Not once did he ever say to himself, "I hated it when she shoved me like that. I shouldn't do that to her, either." He never saw the wrong that he did to me, even though I tried to mirror his behavior. He just never understood; he was never able to see himself.

Physical abuse is typically not limited to the abuser's spouse or partner; everyone in the household becomes a victim. There were times when my husband would put his hand around my stepdaughter's throat and pin her to the wall, choking her. He sometimes shoved her out the door and slammed it on her when she was halfway out the doorway.

One day when he was mad about something, he had my stepdaughter and me pinned up against the kitchen cabinets. He was screaming and cursing at us while punching the cabinet between our heads. We were both crying and yelling, "Stop!" But he didn't stop until he was good and ready to. I always tried to intervene when he was being violent and abusive to my stepdaughter—I knew I could take the abuse better than she could.

Our pets were also victims of his violent tirades. I worked for a veterinarian at the time, and I had adopted several cats and three dogs. He was never abusive to the cats; he really did love them. But one day he hit our largest dog with a belt, and I went ballistic. He never did that again. After that, I was very careful about the dogs. If he was home, I tried to be there. I always preferred his anger to be directed at me.

When I finally left him, I moved to an apartment that would let me have the cats and one dog. I tried to find a place that would allow me to have the cats and three large dogs; but after looking for months, I realized that wasn't going to happen. It was a very hard decision to make, but I kept the youngest dog and tried to find homes for the other two. Our oldest dog was twelve, and the next oldest was ten. I desperately tried to find a permanent home for them—or at least find a foster home. Unfortunately, no one wants to adopt older dogs; they typically come with health problems, which means vet bills.

The day I moved out of our house was very bittersweet for me; on the way to my new apartment, I had to stop at the vet's office and euthanize my two older dogs. But I would rather have euthanized them than leave them with him and let him beat, mistreat, or neglect them. It was a horrible decision to have to make.

Emotional Abuse

Emotional abuse can include name-calling, saying or doing things to put the victim down, withholding affection, and more. Before he started abusing me physically, my husband would ask me frequently, "Do you love me?" He might ask me that question in the middle of an argument. If I refused to answer, he would get madder. If I said, "No!" he would be furious.

When he was mad at me, he would call me very degrading names, referring to my female body parts. It was very insulting, hurtful, and demeaning. That type of name-calling lowers your self-esteem and self-worth. I believe my husband had many insecurities that he passed to me through his abuse.

At times, he would make up with me to have sex. Unfortunately, I was gullible and desperately wanted my marriage to work, and I would fall for his tactics. During sex, I would be hopeful that we were going to be OK again, but as soon as it was over, he would call me a f—— b—— or some other insulting name. I look back now and believe that this was the onset of the abuse, long before his violent behavior began. For the last year of our marriage, sex wasn't a part of our relationship.

Abusers never use just one weapon against their victims. If someone is physically abusing you, that person is also likely calling you names, insulting your integrity, and withholding affection. Emotional abuse always accompanies physical abuse.

IV

Isolation Abuse

Isolation abuse comes in many forms. Your partner might isolate you from friends and family, listen in on phone conversations, or even restrict your phone calls; he or she might also restrict or stop you from using mail, e-mail, and social media. An abusive partner might confine you to the house, restrict you to living in one room, or sabotage your vehicle.

My husband loved isolation abuse. When he was mad at me, he would go into the den and slam the door shut. He would keep himself isolated from me for days or weeks, only coming out to eat and use the bathroom. The pets and I used the rest of the house. My stepdaughter—unlike me—was free to go into the den, but she usually stayed in her bedroom, avoiding conflict. The last year of our marriage, we lived like that all the time. There was little interaction between us; when we did interact, it ended in violence.

Sometimes he would threaten to hurt me by hurting things I cared about. That's what he did when I bought a used Honda Civic. It was a red hatchback with a sunroof and low mileage, and it was everything I had ever wanted in a car—it was my dream car. God had intervened and made it possible for me to make the payments. But from the day I brought the car home, he was jealous of me for having it. I don't know why. I had picked it out, gotten it financed, and made the payments on it by myself. But he resented me for having that car.

During one argument, he told me, "I'm going to make sure that little red car never runs again!" Yes, this was the man who had given me a car just to go out with me for one night. That was all I needed to hear. I needed my car! I rode around town and found a church that was on a side road. I asked one of the deacons if I could park my car there at night and leave my bicycle there in the daytime. My plan was to bike the two miles to the church each morning and then drive my car to work. In the evenings, I would reverse the process. The hard part was that I worked a second job from 6:00 p.m. to 1:00 a.m. three nights a week. On those nights, it seemed like a long bike ride home in the dark. But it was worth it. My husband never had the opportunity to sabotage my car. Thank you, Jesus!

Threats

Making threats is a favorite tool of abusers. Their goal is to keep you scared and intimidated. Their other goals are to keep you obedient and prevent you from leaving. To achieve those goals, they make all kinds of threats.

I took every threat that my husband made seriously, and I never forgot them. If I hadn't done that, I might have lost the use of my car. After I had been keeping my car parked at the church for several weeks, my husband said, "You can bring your car home; I won't do anything to it." I did not believe that lie! Thankfully, God never allowed him to find the car.

Take any threat to your person, children, possessions, pets, or vehicles seriously. Abusers are extremely dangerous. If you tell your abuser that you are leaving, and he threatens to find you, take it seriously. You may need to move to another town or state. Some domestic violence shelters will help you to move, change your name, and even replace your vehicle to keep you safe. Depending upon your circumstances and the severity of the threats, you may need to take this route, especially if you have children. I was able to tell my husband that I was leaving with the pets, and he didn't give me a hard time about it. Not all abusers will let you leave, though. You may have to leave suddenly, without his knowing. You may have to leave with only some of your belongings or just the clothes on your back. Clothes and furniture are replaceable. Do what you have to do to be safe rather than sorry.

After I was able to leave my husband, I was very cautious. When I drove down the road, I constantly looked in the rearview mirror to see if he was following me. At work, I watched the cars that pulled in and out of the parking lot. I didn't go shopping at night. When I was at home, I didn't open the door—even in the daytime—unless I was certain I knew who it was. To my knowledge, he never tried to find me.

Financial Abuse

The goal of someone who abuses you financially is to keep you from being able to leave. The abuser wants you to be stuck, with no way out. In my marriage, the financial abuse started slowly and then escalated. My husband and I had a joint checking account. On his way to work every morning, he would stop at a convenience store and write a check for gas, candy bars, cigarettes, and cans of Mountain Dew. Sometimes he would write a check for twenty dollars, and sometimes for forty, possibly more. At the end of the week, we would have two to three hundred dollars in bad checks and bounced check fees. Some months our bounced check fees totaled eight hundred dollars—not counting the written amount of the checks.

Every time a credit card application came in the mail, he demanded that I fill it out, which I did—filling it out was easier than fighting about it. Soon after, we would have another credit card account. Within a few days or weeks, we would have charged the maximum amount to the new account. Sometimes, we even had to pay overage fees.

When we couldn't pay the bills, it was my fault. When the utility company cut off our utilities, it was my fault. When the phone rang off the hook with creditors trying to collect, it was my fault. Everything was always my fault.

During this time, I worked two jobs. I was paid well to work full time as a veterinary assistant, and I worked three nights a week at the pet ER in Huntsville. Many times, I tried to get him to help me make a budget so that we could manage our money. I would tell him, "You need to stop writing bad checks. We need to put money aside each week to pay the bills at the end of the month." But he refused to stop. His opinion was that I needed to estimate how much he spent every day. It wasn't convenient for him to record the checks in the checkbook register, and he refused to stop spending money we didn't have. One day, after I refused to work on the checkbook register with him anymore, he said, "You are trying to make me be responsible, and it's NOT going to happen!" He was determined to sabotage our finances. After that, I had a separate checking account, and we divided the bills between us.

My new checking account only worked for a few months before he came up with another way to abuse me financially. He started making me responsible for more and more of the household bills. Finally, I realized that I was paying ALL of the household bills except the house payment. It was hard. After I paid all the bills, I had only enough money to buy gas to go back and forth to work.

Of course, he still wasn't going to be satisfied unless I began contributing to the house payment. When he demanded that, I refused. He brought home $2,000 a month, but he couldn't pay $550 each month for the house?

During this time, I volunteered two days a week at a domestic violence shelter. The Lord had literally spoken to my spirit about this. It was ironic that I was a volunteer there, since I really needed to be one of the shelter's clients. No one there knew I was living in a domestic violence situation.

One day, after I was paid at the vet hospital, I paid all the bills that I could on my lunch break. I was left with gas money that had to last until my next paycheck. When I got home from work, my husband was in a rage. I don't remember what had set him off, but as soon as I walked in the door, he said, "Do you see all this food in the cabinets and in the refrigerator?" He ran his arm down the length of the cabinets. "Yes," I replied. He said, "This food is not for you! I do not buy food for you to eat! This food is for me and my daughter to eat!" I said, "I wish you had told me that sooner. I would have bought food for myself. I only have gas money." He yelled, "Tough! I don't buy food for you to eat! I had better not catch you in any of the cabinets or in the refrigerator ever again!" I was devastated. I didn't have money to buy food. I finally decided that I could buy a bag of pinto beans, which cost about a dollar, and make a pot of beans to last until I was paid again. I would need to manage my money better so that I could feed myself.

The next day was one of the days I was scheduled to work at the domestic violence shelter as a volunteer. When I got there, the manager said to me, "There's a box for you in the office." I thought to myself, "Why would there be a box here for me? Most people don't know I volunteer here. Why would someone send something here?" I went into the office and saw a huge box sitting on the floor. Written on the top of the box was "SHARON'S BLESSINGS BOX." It was from the manager of the domestic violence shelter, and it was full of canned food! It was a miracle from God. No one EXCEPT GOD knew what had happened the night before. No one else knew that my husband had forbidden me to eat any food in the house. Praise God! What a blessing! I wasn't going to have to eat pinto beans every day. From then on, I always kept a supply of canned food in my bedroom.

One day, my husband had the audacity to come into the bedroom and grab some of it. He said, "I don't have money to buy my daughter and myself any food. I'm going to take yours!" I let him; it wasn't worth the fight, and I knew the Bible said to feed your enemies—yes, at that point, I considered him an enemy. I never ate any food out of the refrigerator or cabinets in that house ever again.

I think of this passage in the Bible:

Dear friends, never take revenge. Leave that to the righteous anger of God. For the scriptures say, "I will take revenge; I will pay them back," says the Lord. Instead, "if your enemies are hungry, feed them. If they are thirsty, give them something to drink. In doing this, you will heap burning coals of shame on their heads." (Romans 12:19–20 NLT)

Property Abuse

Property abuse can consist of anything from punching walls and pounding tables to breaking down doors and smashing things. To tell about how property abuse affected me, I have to tell the story of my search for a guitar. My husband's financial abuse had forced the two of us to file for bankruptcy, but we were able to keep the house and our vehicles. It was during this time that I prayed God would give me a guitar that was a testimony to Him—a guitar so anointed that I wouldn't even have to play it; people could look at it and see that it was from God. I went to all the music stores in Huntsville looking for *the* guitar.

Usually, when you go into a music store, you see guitars hanging on the wall with price tags hanging from their necks. I always check the price, and if it's out of my range, I don't even take the guitar off the wall. The last music store I went to had *the* guitar, but there was no price tag on it. I'd decided that I could spend about $1,000 on a layaway plan. This guitar looked so awesome—even though I didn't know the price, I had to play it. I sat down on a stool and started playing. It fit me like a glove, and it sounded like a dream!

After about ten minutes or so of playing this awesome guitar, the salesperson came over and asked if I needed help. "Yes," I said, "How much is this guitar?" He left for a few minutes to find out about the price. When he came back, he said, "It's $2,100 with the case." I was so mad! I jumped off the stool and put the guitar back where it had hung on the wall. I told him,

"If there had been a price tag on it, I never would've played it! I can't afford that!" I left the store praying that if God wanted me to have it, He would make it possible.

The guitar stayed on my mind. No matter how hard I tried, I couldn't stop thinking about it. After about three days, I asked the Lord if He wanted me to step out in faith and put the guitar on layaway. He said, "YES!" I took an old twelve-string guitar that I had and didn't like, and I used it as a down payment on my new guitar. They valued the twelve-string at $200. God had ninety days to pay the new guitar off.

That $200 trade-in allowance was literally the only money I paid on the new guitar. When I was at a store shopping, someone would come up to me and say, "God told me to give this to you," and would hand me money. I would go to church, come home, read my Bible, and find money in it. Every time God blessed me with extra money, I used it to pay what I owed on the new guitar. I didn't get an income tax refund that year, and I didn't receive an inheritance either. Instead, God had people giving me money—and most of them were people I didn't even know!

Five days before God paid off the guitar, I had a dream. In the dream, I saw large hands handing me seven one-hundred-dollar bills. Five days later, someone handed me seven one-hundred-dollar bills! In forty-five days, the guitar was paid off. God paid for every bit of it!

Was my husband happy for me? No, he wasn't. In fact, he was very jealous—and very angry. He would say, "If God paid your guitar off, why doesn't He pay the house off? Why won't He pay my truck off?" Then he would get very nasty and say, "I think you went out and begged people to give you that money!" No, I never asked anyone for a dime.

The new guitar really got under my husband's skin. He simply couldn't stand it! One day, in yet another argument, he said, "I'm going to take that guitar of yours and pawn it." He grabbed the case and headed for the door. I told him, "You go right ahead and leave with my guitar. You won't get to the end of the driveway before God knocks you out!" God wasn't going to allow him to pawn my blessing. My husband knew I meant it, and he put the guitar back. After that, he would threaten to take it, but he never again touched my guitar. Somehow, he knew better. As Psalm 105:15 (King James Version) says, "Touch not my anointed, and do my prophets no harm."

I can't tell you how many times my husband punched walls and cabinets or smashed things. One time our car wouldn't start, and he wanted me to push it down the hill while he sat in the driver's seat popping the clutch and trying to jump start the engine. When it turned out that I wasn't strong enough to push the car down the hill, he punched the windshield out. We not only had to pay a mechanic to fix the car, we also had to buy a new windshield.

Verbal Abuse

Someone who verbally abuses you curses you and accuses you of things you didn't do. The abuser may use your past to control and manipulate you, or make unreasonable demands of you. Almost every abusive situation includes a verbal component. I think I have been called b—— more than I have been called by my name, especially when I was younger.

When I was a child—and throughout my adult life—my mother would often say, "Sharon, I am going to murder you!" That was her answer for everything that upset her. I was so used to hearing it that it never crossed my mind that she was actually talking about killing me. In her mind, she may have been saying it in jest or exaggerating to make a point, but I believe these are serious words and are not to be taken lightly.

I believe that when people call you names they don't think very much of themselves. When people put you down, they are trying to make themselves look better than you. They try to make themselves look like geniuses while you look like the biggest idiot on the planet.

This is what God says about someone who verbally abuses you:

Claiming to be wise, they instead became utter fools. And instead of worshiping the glorious, ever-living God, they worshiped idols made to look like mere people and birds and animals and reptiles. (Rom. 1:22–23 NLT)

The fear of the Lord is the beginning of wisdom, and the knowledge of the Holy One is understanding. (Prov. 9:10 NIV)

How true that scripture in Romans is. Typically, people who like to show off their intelligence are ignorant fools; nobody knows everything. Most know-it-alls are arrogant: you can't tell them anything if they already know it all! We should pity people like that; typically, they are abusers.

The scripture in Proverbs says that fearing the Lord is the *beginning* of wisdom. Wisdom begins in us when we respect the Lord. It's not about our intelligence or upbringing; it's not about our education. It's about respecting the Lord and His Word. When you do that, wisdom comes.

⊘ ℋ

We are All Equal in God's Eyes

Some men love to act as if women are inferior to them. Even these days, some men try to keep women "in their place." But God instilled gifts, talents, and intelligence in women, just as he instilled them in men.

In Genesis 2, we are told that God created birds, animals, livestock, and wild animals. He brought them to Adam to name, and Adam "gave names to all the livestock, all the birds of the sky, and all the wild animals. But still there was no helper just right for him. (Gen. 2:20 NLT)

God gave intelligence and wisdom to animals. Each of the different species has its own language, whether they hoot, quack, neigh, bark, or meow. But none of these animals was a good enough helper to Adam. None of these animals could help him mow the grass or work in the fields; none of these animals could speak Adam's language or voice an opinion on important matters. No, God created woman to be everything that Adam needed in a helper.

> So the Lord God caused the man to fall into a deep sleep. While the man slept, the Lord God took out one of the man's ribs and closed up the opening. Then the Lord God made a woman from the rib, and He brought her to the man. "At last!" the man exclaimed. "This one is bone from my bone, and flesh from my flesh! She will be called 'woman,' because she was taken from 'man.'" (Gen. 2:21–23 NIV)

Matthew Henry says, "Women were created from the rib of man to be beside him, not from his head to top him, nor from his feet to be trampled by him, but from under his arm to be protected by him, near to his heart to be loved by him." I also believe women were created from the rib of man because we are equal to men. We are told,

> One day a petition was presented by the daughters of Zelophehad—Mahlah, Noah, Hoglah, Milcah, and Tirza. Their father, Zelophehad, was a son of Hepher, son of Gilead, son of Makir, son of Manasseh, son of Joseph. These women stood before Moses, Eleazar the priest, the tribal leaders, and the entire community at the entrance of the Tabernacle. "Our father died in the wilderness," they said. "He was not among Korah's followers, who rebelled against the Lord; he died because of his own sin. But he had no sons. Why should the name of our father disappear from his clan just because he had no sons? Give us property along with the rest of our relatives."
>
> So Moses brought their case before the Lord. And the Lord replied to Moses, "The claim of the daughters of Zelophehad is legitimate. You must give them a grant of land along with their father's relatives. Assign them the property that would have been given to their father.
>
> "And give the following instructions to the people of Israel: If a man dies and has no son, then give his inheritance to his daughters. And if he has no daughter either, transfer his inheritance to his brothers. If he has no brothers, give his inheritance to his father's brothers. But if his father has no brothers, give his inheritance to the nearest relative in his clan. This is a legal requirement for the people of Israel, just as the Lord commanded Moses." (Num. 27:1–27 NLT)

Zelophedad's daughters wanted their inheritance. These four brave women went before Moses, the priest, the leaders, and the entire community to ask for their father's inheritance. In those days, when a father died, everything he owned automatically went to his sons. Since Zelophedad didn't have any sons, the daughters—rightfully—wanted their father's land.

When Moses prayed about the matter, God let him know that the daughters were right. They SHOULD receive their father's land as an inheritance. I believe that if God felt that women were too stupid to manage the land, He would not have allowed them to claim the property.

An abusive husband's goal is to brainwash you into believing that you can't make it in the world without him. He constantly lets you know that you are incompetent as a wife and mother, that you can't drive the car without destroying it, that you don't clean house well, that you can't cook and clean, and that you can't manage money. An abusive man wants you to wonder how you ever made it in this world before you married him. He wants you to think that everything you say is stupid, and he loves to act as if you are the biggest idiot that has ever been born. Unfortunately, this sort of brainwashing also happens outside of marriage.

Sadly, women still receive less pay than men for doing the same job. Even in the church community, some congregations won't allow a woman to preach or be a leader. Some churches only allow women to clean the restrooms, organize potlucks, and teach the children—somehow, they think we are smart enough to do that.

But women are just as anointed, gifted, and intelligent as men are. Let's look at Deborah:

> Deborah, the wife of Lappidoth, was a prophet who was judging Israel at that time. She would sit under the Palm of Deborah, between Ramah and Bethel in the hill country of Ephraim, and the Israelites would go to her for judgment. One day she sent for Barak son of Abinoam, who lived in Kedesh in the land of Naphtali. She said to him, "This is what the Lord, the God of Israel, commands you: Call out ten thousand warriors from the tribes of Naphtali and Zebulun at Mount Tabor. And I will call out Sisera, commander of Jabin's army, along with his chariots and warriors, to the Kishon River. There I will give you victory over him."
>
> Barak told her, "I will go, but only if you go with me."
>
> "Very well," she replied, "I will go with you. But you will receive no honor in this venture, for the Lord's victory over Sisera will be at

the hand of a woman." So Deborah went with Barak to Kedesh. At Kedesh, Barak called together the tribes of Zebulun and Naphtali, and ten thousand warriors went up with him. Deborah also went with him.

Now Heber the Kenite, a descendant of Moses' brother-in-law Hobab, had moved away from the other member of his tribe and pitched his tent by the oak of Zaanannim near Kedesh.

When Sisera was told that Barak, son of Abinoam, had gone up to Mount Tabor, he called for all nine hundred of his iron chariots and all of his warriors, and they marched from Harosheth-haggoyim to the Kishon River.

Then Deborah said to Barak, "Get ready! This is the day the Lord will give you victory over Sisera, for the Lord is marching ahead of you." So Barak led his ten thousand warriors down the slopes of Mount Tabor into battle. When Barak attacked, the Lord threw Sisera and all his chariots and warriors into a panic. Sisera leaped down from his chariot and escaped on foot. Then Barak chased the chariots and the enemy army all the way to Harosheth-haggoyim, killing all of Sisera's warriors. Not a single one was left alive.

Meanwhile, Sisera ran to the tent of Jael, the wife of Heber the Kenite, because Heber's family was on friendly terms with King Jabin of Hazor. Jael went out to meet Sisera and said to him, "Come into my tent, sir. Come in. Don't be afraid." So he went into her tent, and she covered him with a blanket.

"Please give me some water," he said. "I'm thirsty." So she gave him some milk from a leather bag and covered him again.

"Stand at the door of the tent," he told her. "If anybody comes and asks you if there is anyone here, say no."

But when Sisera fell asleep from exhaustion, Jael quietly crept up to him with a hammer and tent peg in her hand. Then she drove the tent peg through his temple and into the ground, and so he died.

When Barak came looking for Sisera, Jael went out to meet him. She said, "Come, and I will show you the man you are looking for."

So he followed her into the tent and found Sisera lying there dead, with the tent peg through his temple.

So on that day Israel saw God defeat Jabin, the Canaanite king. And from that time on Israel became stronger and stronger against King Jabin until they finally destroyed him. (Judges 4:4–24 NIV)

Deborah had many qualities. It's obvious that she loved God and was faithful to Him. The Bible does not say how Deborah ended up becoming the ruler over Israel, but she did. This was God's chosen appointment for her. She was similar to King Solomon in that people came to hear the wisdom that God had instilled in her. She was a prophetess, and the fifth Judge in Israel. She was a fearless warrior, not afraid to defeat the most dangerous of foes, and she was also a songwriter. Judges 5 is the song that Deborah wrote to praise the Lord for victory in battle.

Women were subordinate to men at the time, yet Deborah's husband is only mentioned once. He must have been a man who was very comfortable with who he was and very comfortable with the fact that his wife was a leader while he was not. Maybe he was a behind-the-scenes kind of guy. Most men, even today, would have a problem with their wife's having so much authority, bravery, wisdom, and such a close relationship with God. Most men would feel intimidated by her or feel that they were in competition with her.

Deborah is to be admired because she didn't change who she was. I'm sure there were men who called her bad names behind her back. They might have called her "bossy" because of her job and gifts. Some women hide their intelligence to make men feel better about themselves. Deborah didn't do that. She used her gifts, talents, and wit to the fullest, and she made no apologies for it. More women should be like Deborah.

Getting Out

Getting out and getting away from your abuser is never easy. As a woman, I desperately wanted to leave and end the abuse; as a Christian, I wanted my marriage to work.

When you're in an abusive situation, it's very hard to think clearly. What should be logical suddenly doesn't seem logical. Your life is a roller coaster ride. Have you ever been on a roller coaster and tried to think about what bills you need to pay next week? Probably not. No, you need to wait for the ride to stop so you can think clearly. Living in a domestic violence situation is like being on a roller coaster. But matters are worse because you have been verbally, emotionally, and physically battered.

When I was still married to my abusive husband, I counseled with my pastor. He gave me bad advice, and because of that, I stayed in my marriage two years longer than I should have. My pastor would say, "God hates divorce" or "If you leave your husband, the church will NOT stand behind you!" The worst advice of all was this: "Sharon, just go home and LOVE your husband." So I would go home and get yelled and cussed at and smacked around.

In answer to my pastor's responses—yes, God does hate divorce. The Bible says that. But my pastor only quoted part of the scripture. Other parts of scripture are relevant:

"I hate divorce," says the Lord God of Israel, "and I hate a man's covering himself with violence as well as with his garment," says the Lord Almighty. (Malachi 2:16, NIV)

One night, after a prayer service, God let me know it was OK to leave my marriage. I read in the Bible:

But he said to me, "My grace is sufficient for you, for my power is made perfect in weakness." Therefore I will boast all the more gladly about my weaknesses, so that Christ's power may rest on me. (2 Corinthians 12:9, NIV)

That was all I needed to hear. God was going to be with me wherever I went. I told God right then, "I'm leaving and divorcing him." I finally had peace. A few days later, when I saw my pastor again, I told him, "I'm divorcing my husband. You and the church do what you have to do." He looked at me for a moment and said, "OK, we will stand behind you."

Every situation is different, just as every abuser is different. I prayed about the best and safest way to leave, and then I divorced him BEFORE I left. I did that because I knew my address would be on the divorce papers; I let that address be with him.

After I moved out, it took a long time before I felt safe. Every knock on the door sent chills up my spine. I diligently watched for his car in my rearview mirror. I scanned the parking lot at work and looked for it wherever I went. But as time went on, the fear I felt went away.

Becoming Independent

Becoming independent begins before you leave. You have to plan a safe, permanent escape, and you have to make a financial plan. I personally believe it is vitally important that your abuser NOT know where you are going to live. In more extreme situations, it is best that he not know where you are working—it may even be best for you to move to another town or state. If you have children, talk with your lawyer before leaving, especially if you intend to move out of state. You don't need to violate your abuser's parental rights and get yourself in legal trouble.

I prepared for almost a year before I left. I opened my own checking account and saved every extra bit of money that I could. I paid off the bills I was able to pay off. I also researched how much rent would be—including security, pet, and utility deposits. The utilities were in my name at the house I had lived in with my abuser-husband, so we had to meet at the utility company to remove my name from the account; he had to sign and accept responsibility for paying the bill.

You need to go over all the bills that you and your abuser are jointly responsible for and see what needs to be done. It's easy to remove your name from some accounts; making a change just requires a signature. Removing your name from other accounts is a little more difficult. It may take some time, but do the best you can to get all your finances in order so you are more prepared to handle things when you leave. But if you are in a crisis, don't wait! Just leave, and get your finances in order later.

The freedom you feel when you leave will make you feel a little nervous. I worried about my abuser finding me; I also worried about paying all my bills every month. In the end, it wasn't a problem. When God is with you, as He was with me, He will make a way.

Consider these verses from scripture:

And this same God who takes care of me will supply all your needs from His glorious riches, which have been given to us in Christ Jesus. (Phil. 4:19 NLT)

The Lord is my shepherd; I have all that I need. He lets me rest in green meadows; He leads me beside peaceful streams. He renews my strength. He guides me along right paths, bringing honor to His name. Even when I walk through the darkest valley, I will not be afraid, for You are close beside me. Your rod and Your staff protect and comfort me. You prepare a feast for me in the presence of my enemies. You honor me by anointing my head with oil. My cup over-flows with blessings. Surely Your goodness and unfailing love will pursue me all the days of my life, and I will live in the house of the Lord forever. (Ps. 23:1–6 NLT)

These are about God keeping you safe:

You can go to bed without fear; you will lie down and sleep soundly. (Proverbs 3:24 NLT)

You will lie down unafraid, and many will look to you for help. (Job 11:19 NLT)

But all who listen to me will live in peace, untroubled by fear of harm. (Prov. 1:33 NLT)

The longer you are away from your abuser, the more you will feel safe, and the more you will realize you can make it in this world without him. More and more, you will feel independent and free. It is never God's will for someone to be abused in any way: do not allow anyone to tell you any differently. Stand on the Word of God. It is written in John 8:36: "So if the Son sets you free, you are truly free."

I always recommend that someone planning a move into a new home anoint the home first. I've sometimes had the moving van sitting in the driveway while I waited for a few people from church to come and help me pray. This is a very simple thing to do and only takes about ten minutes, but it is well worth your time.

Gather a few good Christians, take some anointing oil, and go around the house praying and putting oil on the doors and windows. Cast out all the demons that have been allowed to stay there, and let them know that this place is now a temple of the Holy Spirit. Then pray that anyone who goes in or out of the doors and windows will be saved. Pray that no demon will even try to cross the boundary line. If you have a yard, walk the property line, scattering drops of olive oil and praying that no one with evil intent will cross it. Take authority over your new home in Jesus's name. We are told,

> These miraculous signs will accompany those who believe: They will cast out demons in My name, and they will speak in new languages. They will be able to handle snakes with safety, and if they drink anything poisonous, it won't hurt them. They will be able to place their hands on the sick, and they will be healed. (Mark 16:17–18 NLT)
>
> I tell you the truth, whatever you forbid on earth will be forbidden in heaven, and whatever you permit on earth will be permitted in heaven. I also tell you this: If two of you agree here on earth concerning anything you ask, My Father in heaven will do it for you. For where two or three gather together as My followers, I am there among them. (Matt. 18:18–19 NLT)
>
> And I will give you the keys of the Kingdom of Heaven. Whatever you forbid on earth will be forbidden in heaven, and whatever you permit on earth will be permitted in heaven. (Matt. 16:19 NLT)
>
> Behold, I give unto you power to tread on serpents and scorpions, and over all the power of the enemy: and nothing shall by any means hurt you. (Luke 10:19, KJV)

It is also good to speak Psalm 91, the psalm of protection, over your home and yourself.

> Those who live in the shelter of the Most High will find rest in the shadow of the Almighty. This I declare about the Lord: He alone is my refuge, my place of safety; He is my God, and I trust Him. For He will rescue you from every trap and protect you from deadly disease. He will cover you with His feathers. He will shelter you with His wings. His faithful promises are your armor and protection. Do not be afraid of the terrors of the night, nor the arrow that flies in the day. Do not dread the disease that stalks in darkness, nor the disaster that strikes at midday. Though a thousand fall at your side, though ten thousand are dying around you, these evils will not touch you. Just open your eyes, and see how the wicked are punished. If you make the Lord your refuge, if you make the Most High your shelter, no evil will conquer you; no plague will come near your home. For He will order His angels to protect you wherever you go. They will hold you up with their hands so you won't even hurt your foot on a stone. You will trample upon lions and cobras; you will crush fierce lions and serpents under your feet! The Lord says, "I will rescue those who love Me. I will protect those who trust in My name. When they call on Me, I will answer; I will be with them in trouble. I will rescue and honor them. I will reward them with a long life and give them My salvation." (Ps. 91:1–16 NLT)

✿❦✿

Get a Life!

In my marriage, I lost myself. I had to give up the things I loved to do in order to keep my abuser happy. When I finally left and started to get a life again, I realized that I wasn't sure who I was anymore. I had become a mere shadow of the person I had been—and the person God intended me to be. I had to find myself again. I picked up some of my old hobbies and interests, and I also discovered some new ones. In some ways, I am similar to my old self, but I am different. I am a new and improved version of Sharon. I found victory by speaking the Word of God over myself.

> It is the same with My Word. I send it out, and it always produces fruit. It will accomplish all I want it to, and It will prosper everywhere I send it. (Isa. 55:11 NLT)

In Ezekiel 37, God told Ezekiel to speak a prophetic message to the dry bones.

> Then He said to me, "Speak a prophetic message to these bones and say, 'Dry bones, listen to the Word of the Lord! This is what the Sovereign Lord says: "Look! I am going to put breath into you and make you live again! I will put flesh and muscles on you and cover you with skin. I will put breath into you, and you will come to life. Then you will know that I am the Lord."'" (Ezek. 37:4–6 NLT)

What areas of your life do you want to resurrect from the dead? What part of you was lost in an abusive relationship? You can speak the verses from Ezekiel to put breath into your life.

Here's an example of what to say: "Dry bones of finances, hobbies, self-esteem, healthy relationships, and so on—listen to the Word of the Lord! This is what the Sovereign Lord says: 'Look! I am going to put breath into you and make you live again! I will put flesh and muscles on you and cover you with skin. I WILL PUT BREATH INTO YOU, AND YOU WILL COME TO LIFE. Then you will know that I am the Lord.' I command these areas of my life to rise and be healed and be made whole in the mighty name of Jesus!"

Your abuser wanted to keep you down, to make you feel worthless and useless. You were not created to be someone's emotional or physical punching bag. God created you to be a blessing to those around you. You are anointed, gifted, talented, and intelligent. You have a divine purpose. It is written in Romans 11:29, "For God's gifts and His call are irrevocable" (NIV).

A great way to resurrect the blessed woman within you is to read Proverbs 31 and speak it over your life daily. The woman spoken of in Proverbs 31 is a strong woman of God. She has a good moral standard and is brave and courageous. She is trustworthy and does good. She is a professional dressmaker, and she gets up early to prepare for the day ahead. She owns her own land, and she purchases things with her own money. She is a business owner and hard worker, yet she always has time to help the poor. She takes care of her household. She speaks with wisdom and kindness while giving instructions. She does not tolerate laziness and makes sure the members of her family have responsibilities around the house. She fears the Lord. She doesn't need to brag about herself; her work is her reward. YOU are the kind of woman spoken about in Proverbs 31:

Who can find a virtuous and capable wife? She is more precious than rubies. Her husband can trust her, and she will greatly enrich his life. She brings him good, not harm, all the days of her life. She finds wool and flax and busily spins it. She is like a merchant's ship, bringing her food from afar. She gets up before dawn to prepare breakfast for her household and plan the day's work for her servant girls. She goes to inspect a field and buys it; with her earnings, she plants a vineyard. She is energetic and strong, a hard worker. She makes sure her dealings are profitable; her lamp burns late into the night. Her hands are busy spinning thread, her fingers twisting fiber. She extends a helping hand to the poor and opens her arms to the needy. She has no fear of winter for her household, for everyone has warm clothes. She makes her own bedspreads. She dresses in fine linen and purple gowns. Her husband is well known at the city gates, where he sits with the other civic leaders. She makes belted linen garments and sashes to sell to the merchants. She is clothed with strength and dignity, and she laughs without fear of the future. When she speaks, her words are wise, and she gives instructions with kindness. She carefully watches everything in her household and suffers nothing from laziness. Her children stand and bless her. Her husband praises her: "There are many virtuous and capable women in the world, but you surpass them all!" Charm is deceptive, and beauty does not last; but a woman who fears the Lord will be greatly praised. Reward her for all she has done. Let her deeds publicly declare her praise. (Prov. 31:10–31 NLT)

Conclusion:

Once I was able to get away and start my life over, God really moved in my life. I divorced my abuser in April of 2003, and on November 22, 2003, the Rose of Sharon Soup Kitchen and Thrift Store ministry opened. If I had remained with my abuser, this ministry would never have existed. My abuser repeatedly told me that I wasn't hearing from God; he mocked me and everything that God said to my heart. The visions that God showed me were a joke to him. I wonder if he's still laughing now.

Many times, the devil uses the people closest to you to stop you from doing God's will, to stop you from prospering. Don't listen to them; listen to God. Jesus wants to bless you and to prosper you. Jesus wants you to enjoy your life. But it's hard for the Lord to raise you up into the person He wants you to be when someone is beating you down. Do your daily prayer time and Bible study time; listen to what He is telling you. Ask Him how He wants you to get out, and where He wants you to go. God has all the answers for your life. Trust Him.

About the Author

Sharon Rose Walker is the founder and CEO of the Rose of Sharon Soup Kitchen and Thrift Store in Huntsville, Alabama. She received Jesus Christ as her Savior in 1994 and entered full-time ministry in 2001. Walker graduated from Notre Dame College in 1981 with a degree in music performance.

CPSIA information can be obtained
at www.ICGtesting.com
Printed in the USA
LVOW08s0038091116
512211LV00007B/151/P